CRAYOLA TUNDRA COLORS

Lisa Bullard

Lerner Publications ◆ Minneapolis

For Joel

Lerner Publications Company
An imprint of Lerner Publishing Group, Inc.
241 First Avenue North
Minneapolis, MN 55401 USA

For reading levels and more information, look up this title at www.lernerbooks.com.

Main body text set in Mikado a. Typeface provided by HVD fonts.

Editor: Jordyn Taylor **Designer:** Viet Chu

Library of Congress Cataloging-in-Publication Data

Names: Bullard, Lisa, author.
Title: Crayola tundra colors / Lisa Bullard.
Description: Minneapolis : Lerner Publications, [2021] | Series: Crayola colorful biomes | Includes bibliographical references and index. | Audience: Ages 5–9 | Audience: Grades K–1 | Summary: "Orange lichens, brown caribou, and flashy fish are just some of the colorful things found in the tundra. Readers discover fascinating facts about the range of life that thrives in this beautiful place"— Provided by publisher.
Identifiers: LCCN 2019047556 (print) | LCCN 2019047557 (ebook) | ISBN 9781541577534 (library binding) | ISBN 9781728413136 (paperback) | ISBN 9781541599826 (ebook)
Subjects: LCSH: Tundra animals—Color—Juvenile literature. | Tundra plants—Color—Juvenile literature.
Classification: LCC QL105 .B85 2020 (print) | LCC QL105 (ebook) | DDC 591.75/86—dc23

LC record available at https://lccn.loc.gov/2019047556
LC ebook record available at https://lccn.loc.gov/2019047557

Manufactured in the United States of America
1-46776-47767-2/6/2020

Table of Contents

Welcome to the Tundra

Brrr! This cold biome is the tundra.

It's a hard place to survive. But some colorful living things find a way.

What Is the Tundra?

The tundra is an area where tall trees can't grow.

It gets little rain or snow. It's often cold. Many animals leave for the long winters.

NORTH AMERICA

☐ TUNDRA

EUROPE

ASIA

AFRICA

SOUTH
AMERICA

AUSTRALIA

The Arctic tundra is far north. It's near the Arctic ice caps. The ground stays frozen most of the year.

Alpine tundra
can be found
near the tops of
high mountains.

Tundra Plants

Tundra plants are short and tough! Strong winds scatter fluffy white cotton grass seeds.

Animals eat ripe, **red** berries.

Purple and **yellow** flowers draw pollinators in the summer.

Biome Fact

Arctic poppy flowers turn to follow the sun's path.

Bright **orange** sunburst lichen spreads out on a rock.

Zoom Out
The sunburst lichen gets more colorful in the sun.

Big Tundra Animals

Polar bear fur looks **white** but is actually clear.

Biome Fact

Polar bears have black skin under their fur. The dark color helps them take in more sunlight.

Musk oxen have fluffy, dark **brown** outer coats.

Snow leopards' spotted **tan**-and-**gray** coats help them blend in. They stay hidden while hunting.

Some tundra animals change color with the seasons. Peary caribou turn mostly white for winter.

The arctic fox turns **brown** in the summer.

Small Tundra Animals

The **olive-green** kea flashes **scarlet** feathers when it flies.

Biome Fact

The kea is the only parrot in the tundra.

The **gold**-and-**black** colors of Arctic bumblebees warn away predators.

American pikas are rusty **brown** or gray. Their color helps them hide from predators.

Male monal birds use their bright colors to attract females. Look at the **black**, **blue**, and **orange**!

Zoom In

Himalayan monals have a crest of shiny **green** feathers on their head.

Some tundra animals change color during mating season. Male moor frogs turn **blue**.

The bottom side of the Dolly Varden fish turns bright **coral**.

Many Colors

The tundra is full of color. Here are some of the Crayola® crayon colors used in this book.

Outrageous Orange

Mahogany

Goldenrod

Periwinkle

Olive Green

Turquoise Blue

29

Glossary

attract: to draw something in or make it interested

clear: easily seen through, lacking color or pigment

lichen: a living thing that is made up of algae and fungi growing together but is not a plant or an animal

mating: to join together to produce young

pollinators: animals that move a plant's pollen to help it make seeds

predators: animals that eat other animals

survive: to stay alive

tundra: areas with frozen subsoil where tall trees can't grow

To Learn More

BOOKS

Boothroyd, Jennifer. *Let's Visit the Tundra*. Minneapolis: Lerner
    Publications, 2017.

Hansen, Grace. *Tundra Biome*. Minneapolis: Abdo Kids, 2017.

Johansson, Philip. *The Tundra: Discover This Frozen Biome*. Berkeley
    Heights, NJ: Enslow Elementary, 2015.

WEBSITES

San Diego Zoo Kids: Polar Bear
    https://kids.sandiegozoo.org/animals/polar-bear

Wonderopolis: How Do Arctic Animals Survive in the Cold?
    https://www.wonderopolis.org/wonder/how-do-arctic-animals
    -survive-in-the-cold

Index

Photo Acknowledgments

Image credits: josef knecht/Wikimedia Commons (CC BY 3.0), p. 4; Jeff Foott/Photodisc/Getty Images, p. 5 (flowers); ANGHI/iStock/Getty Images, p. 5 (lichen); Winfried Wisniewski/Photodisc/Getty Images, p. 5 (bird); Jim Brandenburg/Minden Pictures/Newscom, p. 5 (caribou); Laura Westlund/Independent Picture Service, p. 7; Wildnerdpix/iStock/Getty Images, p. 8; andyKRAKOVSKI/iStock/Getty Images, p. 9; Leonid Ikan/iStock/Getty Images, p. 10; John Pennell/iStock/Getty Images, p. 11; Lisa Hupp/USFWS/flickr (public domain), p. 12; Iri_sha/iStock/Getty Images, p. 13; empire331/iStock/Getty Images, p. 14; urbanraven/iStock/Getty Images, p. 15; Dawn Wilson Photography/Moment/Getty Images, p. 16; Bjørn H Stuedal/500px/Getty Images, p. 17; Thorsten Spoerlein/iStock/Getty Images, p. 19; PaulLoewen/iStock/Getty Images, p. 20; ChameleonsEye/Shutterstock.com, p. 22; John Pennell/iStock/Getty Images, p. 23; mlharing/iStock/Getty Images, p. 24 (pika); ShivamJoshi/Shutterstock.com, p. 24 (bird); chris2766/iStock/Getty Images, p. 25; FloWBo/iStock/Getty Images, p. 26; Jeff Mondragon/Alamy Stock Photo, p. 27.

Cover: longtaildog/iStock/Getty Images (landscape); Sandra Leidholdt/Moment/Getty Images (pika); JohnPitcher/iStock/Getty Images (bears); PaulLoewen/iStock/Getty Images (caribou).